Copyright 2019 by Kollibri terre Sonnenblume.
All photos by the author except: childhood snapshots (J. Stolen); author with "Princess" and with Fugz (Nikki Hill); Fugz on farm machinery (Deva).
All rights reserved.

Published in 2019 by Macska Moksha Press
PO Box 301, Cliff NM 88028
macskamoksha.com

Library of Congress Cataloging-in-Publication Data
Sonnenblume, Kollibri terre, 1969-
Never Trust Anyone Who Doesn't Like Cats
ISBN: 978-0-9861881-9-0
1. Pets—Cats. 2. Humor. I. Sonnenblume, Kollibri terre, 1969-. II. Title

Never Trust Anyone Who Doesn't Like Cats

Kollibri terre Sonnenblume

MACSKA MOKSHA PRESS | CLIFF NM USA

Introduction

I'm a lifelong cat lover, literally from the crib. The ones in this book are just some that I've met over the last decade. At the beginning of that time, I was an urban farmer in Portland, Oregon, where we named our gardens after the resident cats. (After all, they spent more time there than anyone else.) Later, we farmed various rural locations in the Pacific Northwest, and cats were a cherished part of life at all of them. The last few years I've been traveling, and the one consistent factor—from city to country, from forest to valley to desert—has been cats.

The second half of this book mostly features the furry inhabitatants of the property in the Gila River valley of New Mexico where I put together this project. Their disproportionate representation is due only to the fact that they were handy, the autumn light was so lovely, and I had use of a good camera—not favoritism, to which I would never dare admit, so help me Bastet.

I hope you enjoy this far-too-brief tribute to our benevolent feline overlords.

this page: two black kittens in Portland, Oregon; opposite: farmcat near Beatty, Oregon

—Chapter 1—
Cats & Humans: The Early Years

The worship of cats by the ancient Egyptians is famous. Some surmise that this deification happened because cats saved the Egyptians from starvation. The Nile River valley at the time was amazingly fertile due to annual flooding and so food could be grown in great abundance but the granaries were infested by rodents. Enter the cat, hunter of rat. When the people of the Pharaohs befriended *Felis sylvestris lybica*, their days of belt-tightening were over. Now there was enough to go around the whole year. Hence the literal elevation of cats onto pedestals. This cultural reverence was carried down to the individual level: when an Egyptian household's feline died, the whole family would shave off their eyebrows. Their tragedy was thus announced publicly and without shame to friends and neighbors in a fashion that was undeniably...um, in-your-face.

Purr-kins; Chimacum, Washington

Fast-forward a few thousand years and the cat's worthiness was no longer as appreciated. During the Dark Ages in Europe the Church somehow got it into its head that cats were "of the devil" and needed to be eradicated. Perhaps bounties were offered; whatever the motivation, many people took up this ridiculous crusade (is there any other kind?) and cats were decimated. What happened next? Rats bred unchecked and spread the Black Plague, killing at least a third of the population of Europe. This is why cats look so smug to this day. "Not so fast," they seem to be saying in response to any treatment that is less-than-deifying. "Remember what happened last time? We do…"

Cosi (RIP); Lucerne, California

The common house cat, *Felis catus*, is a direct descendant of the African wildcat befriended by the Egyptians, *Felis silvestris lybica*. As Elizabeth Marshall Thomas points out in her book, *The Tribe of Tiger*, when humans began storing grain crops, they unintentionally invited in other members of the grassland ecosystem with the harvest; namely, seed-eating rodents—mice, rats, etc.—and rodent-eating predators: cats.

Sylvio (RIP); Sandy, Oregon

As agriculture spread out from the Middle East, cats followed. When ships came into use, many of them bearing grains, rodents and cats got on aboard, too. In this way, the African wildcat spread around the Mediterranean and into Europe, where it interbred with the Forest Wildcat, *Felis silvestris silvestris* (after whom Sylvester the Cat, of Tweety fame, was named). From the beginning, in other words, the driving force for the cat has been opportunism. This motivation has been unfairly maligned up to the present day by misunderstanding humans.

Mauzers (RIP); Brookings harbor, Oregon

According to C.A.W. Guggisberg, in his classic, *Wild Cats of the World*, statues of women holding cats were found at an archaeological site in Haçilar in Asia Minor that dates back nearly 8000 years. Guggisberg hypothesizes that cats arrived in Italy and Greece about 2000 years ago and moved north gradually, being still rare in England until the 10th Century. A dig at a Roman ruin in Austria, dating to the 2nd and 3rd Century, Guggisberg tells us, uncovered bricks with cat footprints on them: "The animal must have walked over the bricks while they were still soft and laid out to await burning, and in so doing it left the earliest evidence of the domestic cat's presence in Central Europe." If you have ever spent time with cats, you won't have any trouble picturing this episode. Was the cat caught in the act by the brick-maker? Was the brick-maker angry or amused? The cat, we can bet, was surely indifferent.

above: "Torti" of the Gila River valley, New Mexico
following: Siamese in Cove, Oregon and Calico in Hydesville, California

mousers at Eloheh Farm outside Newburg, Oregon

Fugz the Farmcat
Jun 2010-Dec 2012

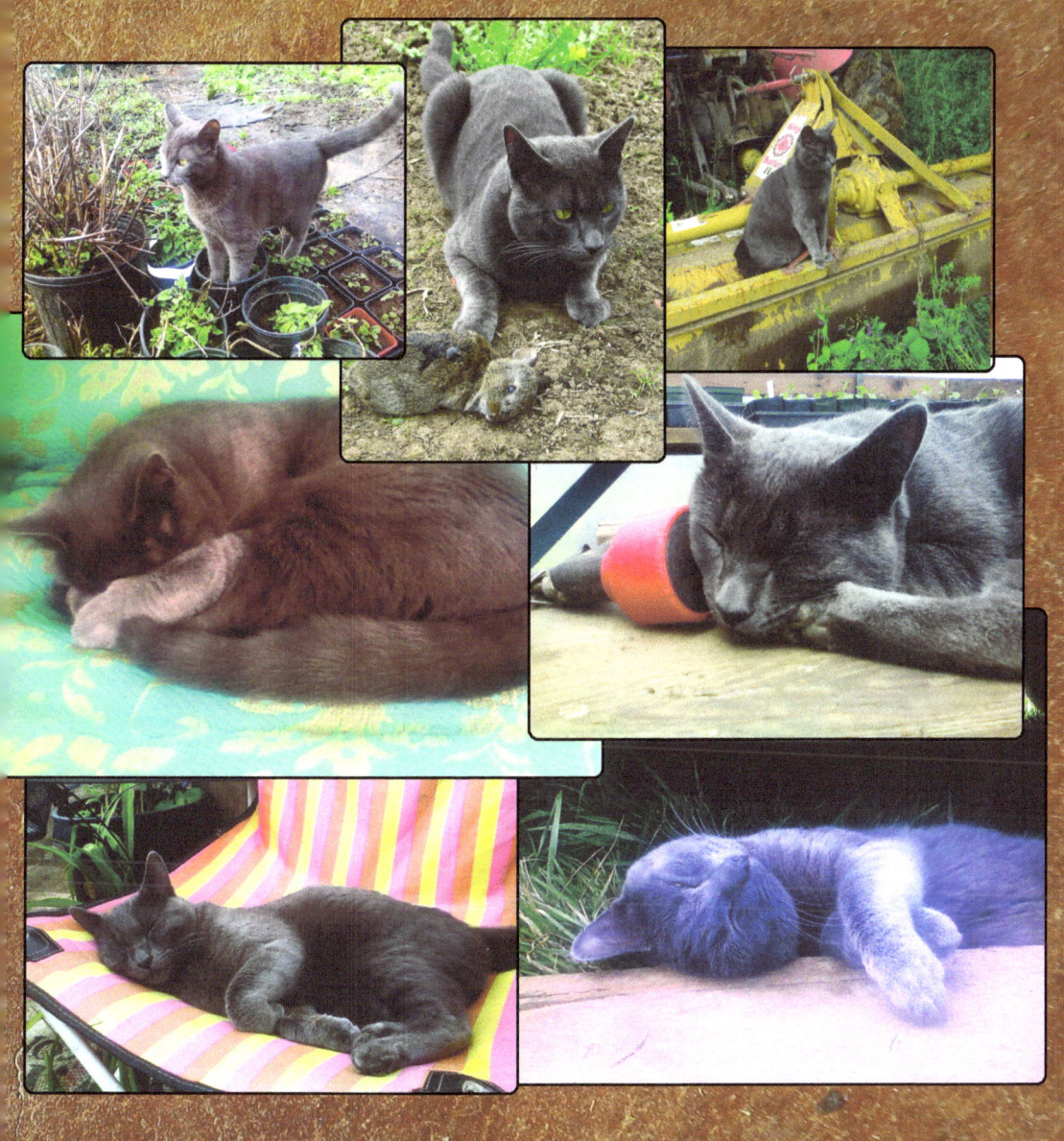

auto parts store cats in Colusa, California

Urban Farming Cats in Portland, Oregon

above: Calvin with a rototiller

starting above:
Shebert, Firepit Cat (with pelt)
Tolman cat (with greens)
Prosperous Calico (with hoe)
Eiskaffeekatze (with Catnip)

following: Spot (RIP); Yucca Valley, California & Dusty Jim; Halfway, Oregon

—Chapter 2—
The Balance of Power

The independent nature of cats has charmed and confounded humans for centuries. For those who prefer the cloying devotion of an over-bred modern dog, subordinated by forced joblessness and confinement, eager to obey commands for treats, a cat can seem stand-offish, finicky, and even stupid. Feline appreciators are more perspicacious, recognizing their companions as discriminating, fastidious and free-spirited.

"Tortie"; Gila River valley in New Mexico

The truth is more stark than that, though, and it is this: Cats simply don't need us. Their entrance into human civilization was of their own free will. If not physically restrained, cats choose their companions and their homes, staying—or going—of their own volition. As Alan Weisman has conjectured in *The World Without Us*, if humans suddenly disappeared from the earth, cats would find their own way, returning to their hunting ways with, if anything, even more success: "Cats will do very well in a world without people who took them to all the continents and islands they didn't already inhabit, where they now outnumber and out-compete other predators their own size."

Sylvio (RIP), in Chimacum, Washington

Not that individual cats are not truly loyal to individual humans. The literature is replete with "Amazing But True Cat Tales" (a delightful book by Bruce Nash & Allan Zullo) that feature journeys of hundreds of miles to be reunited with companions who moved, warnings of imminent danger from intruders or disasters, or simple but profound comforting in times of distress. But such actions are expressions not of codependency but of self-sovereignty. Any love you receive from a cat is *free* love, and is there any other kind?

Shakti; Portland, Oregon

Hence the joy of offering Catnip (*Nepeta cataria*) to cats. They don't need Catnip, but they want it. With Catnip in your hand you can engage a cat in a dance of playful teasing and flirtatious temptation. For a moment the tables are turned and the servant (the human) rises in rank, not to master, but to something approaching equality, which is to say, cat-ness. To be a "Nip Giver" is to attain one of the highest stations in civilized living.

Simon; Portland, Oregon

But for cats, there would be no civilized living. The word "civilization" comes from the Latin, *civilis*, meaning "citizen," and is in turn rooted in the Indo-European *kei*, which connotes "lying down," "bed," and "home," all concepts that quickly bring cats to mind. "Civilized" life emerged from agriculture, and the success of agriculture, as we have seen, was dependent on cats. My own heart is really with anarcho-primitivism (see Zerzan, Glendinning, et al.), but I recoil at the thought of life without cats. What civilization hath wrought—"the wheel, New York, wars and so on" (as Douglas Adams so neatly summed it up in *The Hitchhikers Guide to the Galaxy*)—is truly a mixed bag, to say the least, and in the end will likely be viewed as an unmitigated disaster. In this way of looking at things, cats are both the enabler of our miserable civilization and our consolation prize for having to live in it.

outside the Soda Creek Store at Lake Pillsbury in California

—CHAPTER 3—
THE PROPHECY OF THE CAT MOTHERSHIP

The legend is a simple one: Someday, the Cat Mothership will return to Earth to rescue all the cats from the mess that humans have made of the planet. Only a few people will be allowed to board the Cat Mothership: those who paid **appropriate respect** to *Felis catus* in their lives [their emphasis]. That number will be small.

Cats & kittens looking skyward in the Gila River valley, New Mexico

Will we each be judged before a kitty-cat court, with tail-flicking cross-examinations by prosecutors, purring accolades from defense witnesses, narrow lidded glares from a prosperous long-haired judge and—over there on that sunny window sill—a napping jury? Or will we be scored by a massive maiow-frame computer that tallies every meal served (10 pts), head scratched (3 pts), and nip given (50 pts), as well as every late breakfast (-15 pts), calf-rub demurred (-8 pts), and claim of a "cat allergy" (-375 pts)?

"Silver Mane" of the Gila River valley, New Mexico

Or will the arrival of the Mothership ignite a transcendence of all cats into a single omniscient super-cat-consciousness (if this is not already the case, as some would claim) which will instantaneously beam up the lucky humans, directly into the Mothership kitchen where bowls stand ready to be filled?

Whatever the scenario, we can be sure of one thing: among the humans who are saved, there won't be a single member of the Audubon Society.

Furdi; Portland, Oregon

But what of those who claim to be "allergic to cats"? Isn't that involuntary? My answer: no, not really. I consider the "cat allergy" to be a mental problem, not a physiological one. The condition is the unhappy consequence of cognitive dissonance for the frail, confused human ego: Cats effortlessly embody freedom, independence, and forthrightness, while most human culture institutionalizes coercion, slavishness, and deceit. Some poor humans, experiencing deep consternation, project their inner turbulence onto the blameless cat. This takes shape in a variety of ways: 1) Repressing one's own desire for freedom from a belief that oneself does not deserve it, which is "neurosis"; 2) Oppressing the independence of others in order to dominate, which is "psychopathy"; and 3) Viewing cats as "just animals" with nothing to teach us, which is—clearly—"delusion."

"Little Angel" in the Gila River valley, New Mexico

Not every neurotic, psychopathic or delusional human claims a cat allergy. But nearly everyone suffering this ailment falls into one of those categories. I urge compassion for these poor suffering people and encourage whatever treatment or practice will help them find their way back onto their rockers, which they are clearly off of. Because you know what cats love, and what it is that you lose when you're not sitting down: Your lap!

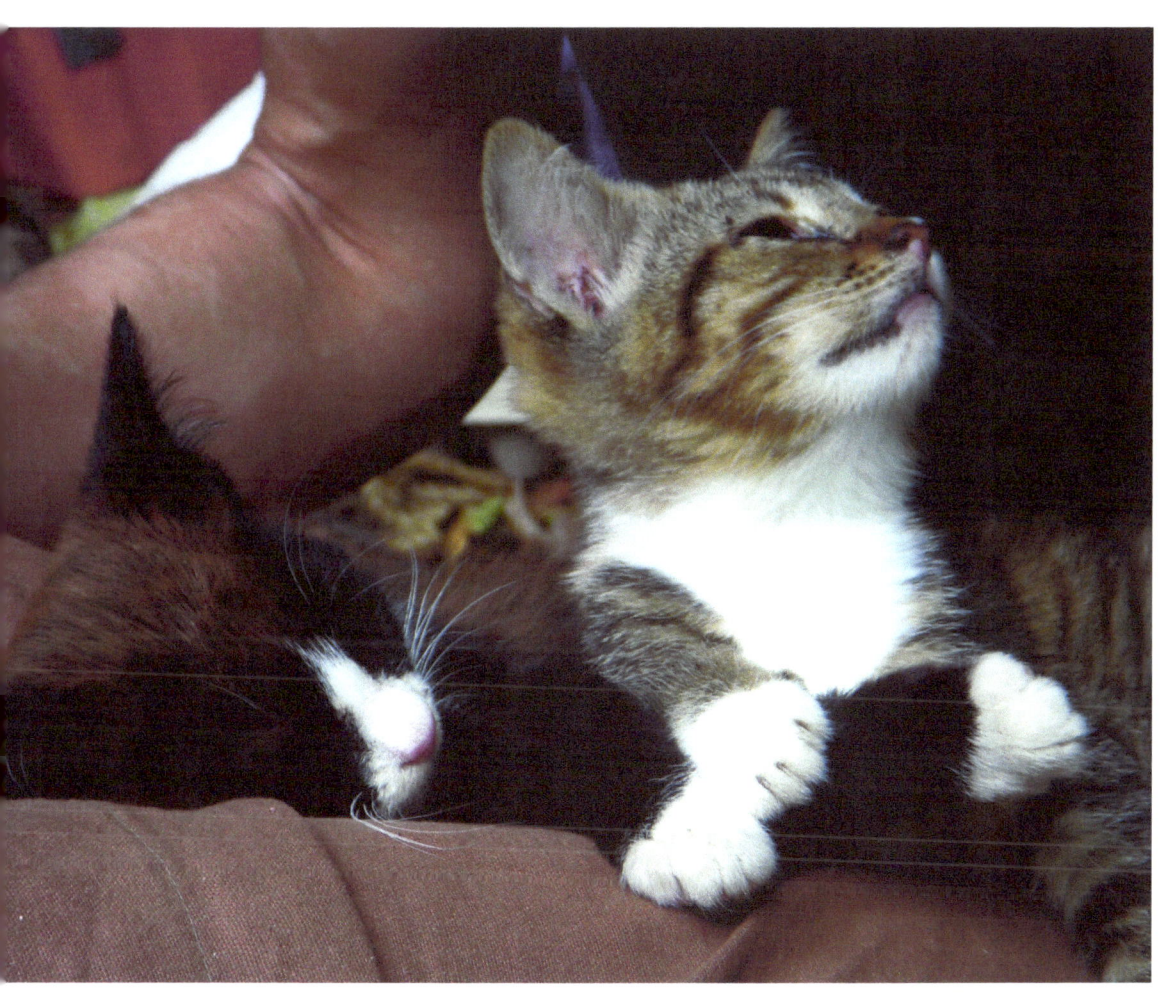

Sylvio (RIP) & Little Bean; Sandy, Oregon

And what of those people who have been actively cruel to cats? The petty cat-kickers? The vicious dog-sickers? The barbarous vivesectionists? Will they get batted around by a cosmic cat brigade 'til their necks are broken and their innards are spilling out? Personally, I wish for it to be worse: that these malicious people will be struck—in heart, mind and soul—with a full awareness of the suffering they caused, and that they will experience it as their own, inescapably, day and night, for the rest of their lives, lives they know will never now include any cat, and hence no chance of redemption. What worse Hell could there be? Oh yeah, and they'll all have to sleep in dirty litter boxes. Forever.

Grey kitten in the Gila River valley, New Mexico

Sometimes I find myself hoping that I will be invited on board the Cat Mothership. But then I remind myself that hope with cats, as with life, is an empty currency. I must simply put myself in their paws, trusting—nay, knowing—that their judgment of me will be fair. After all, who is more of an expert on knowing whether or not their own needs have been satisfied, if not a cat?

Zeus (RIP); Portland, Oregon

Leonard; South Bend, Washington

Thanks to St.At. & Meg for preflight feedback.

Technical notes

This book was created entirely with open-source software. Operating system: Linux Mint 17.1 'Rebecca' and Ubuntu 14.04.5 LTS 'Trusty Tahr;' Software: Scribus 1.4.3.svn, GIMP 2.8, Gwenview 4.14.0 pre, gedit 2.30.4; Laptop from Free Geek in Portland, Oregon: **freegeek.org**.
All fonts public domain/free for commercial use.

Cited works

Adams, Douglas. **The Hitchhikers Guide to the Galaxy** (New York, NY: Del Rey), 1979.
Guggisberg, C.A.W. **Wild Cats of the World** (New York, NY: Taplinger), 1975.
Nash, Bruce & Zullo, Allan. **Amazing But True Cat Tales** (Kansas City, Missouri: Andrews McMeel Publishing), 1993
Thomas, Elizabeth Marshall, Jared Taylor Williams (Illustrator). **The Tribe of Tiger: Cats and Their Culture** (New York, NY: Gallery Books), 1994.
Weisman, Alan. **The World Without Us** (New York, NY: St. Martin's Thomas Dunne Books), 2007.

About the author

The author is a writer, photographer, tree-hugger, animal-lover and cat-worshipper somewhere at large in the western USA. Other works include: **Roadtripping at the End of the World**, **The Failures of Farming & the Necessity of Wildtending**, and **Adventures in Urban Bike Farming**.

See more at Macska Moksha Press:
macskamoksha.com

www.ingramcontent.com/pod-product-compliance
Lightning Source LLC
Chambersburg PA
CBHW041120300426
44112CB00002B/42